JAMAICA BAY PAMPHLET LIBRARY 08

JAMAICA BAY   PHOTO ARCHIVE

STRUCTURES OF COASTAL RESILIENCE
Jamaica Bay Team
Spitzer School of Architecture
The City College of New York

Catherine Seavitt Nordenson, editor
Associate Professor of Landscape Architecture

Kjirsten Alexander
Research Associate

Danae Alessi
Research Associate

Eli Sands
Research Assistant

JAMAICA BAY PAMPHLET LIBRARY
08 Jamaica Bay Photo Archive

ISBN 978-1-942900-08-5

COPYRIGHT

CONTACT

Catherine Seavitt Nordenson
cseavittnordenson@ccny.cuny.edu
www.structuresofcoastalresilience.org

SCR Jamaica Bay Team
The City College of New York
Spitzer School of Architecture
Program in Landscape Architecture, Room 2M24A
141 Convent Avenue New York, New York 10031

COVER

Bicycle and pedestrian path at the Belt Parkway, 1941.
source: New York City Parks Photo Archive. Photo by Rodney McCay Morgan.

supported by

THE ROCKEFELLER FOUNDATION   SCR Structures of Coastal Resilience   CUNY The City University of New York   The City College of New York

JAMAICA BAY   PHOTO ARCHIVE

Parking field and beach at Jacob Riis Park, 1956

source: New York City Parks Photo Archive

Paving the parking field at Jacob Riis Park,1936

source: New York City Parks Photo Archive

New beach retaining wall to be completed at Jacob Riis Park, 1936

source: New York City Parks Photo Archive

Future mall, builiding, and pool site at Jacob Riis Park, 1936

source: New York City Parks Photo Archive

Jacob Riis Park, showing location of future traffic circle, 1936

source: New York City Parks Photo Archive

Cleaning the sand on the beach at Jacob Riis Park, 1937

source: New York City Parks Photo Archive

Old sea wall to be demolished at Jacob Riis Park, 1936

source: New York City Parks Photo Archive

New beach retaining wall to be completed at Jacob Riis Park, 1936

source: New York City Parks Photo Archive

Jacob Riis Park, with Marine Parkway Bridge in background, 1937

source: New York City Parks Photo Archive

Jacob Riis Park, showing old jetties to be removed and replaced, 1936

source: New York City Parks Photo Archive

Belt Parkway parking field at Marine Park / Plumb Beach, with bicycle and pedestrian path, 1941

source: New York City Parks Photo Archive

Bicycle and pedestrian path at the Belt Parkway, 1941

source: New York City Parks Photo Archive. Photo by Rodney McCay Morgan.

East Cross Bay Boulevard Bridge at the Belt Parkway, 1940

source: New York City Parks Photo Archive

Bicycle and pedestrian path at the Belt Parkway, 1941

source: New York City Parks Photo Archive. Photo by Rodney McCay Morgan.

Aerial view of Canarsie Park,1937

source: New York City Parks Photo Archive

Quonset huts built in Canarsie as temporary housing for veterans, 1946

source: Brooklyn Public Library--Brooklyn Collection

Aerial view of Flatbush Avenue and Floyd Bennett Field, looking east toward Canarsie, 1937

source: New York City Parks Photo Archive

Rolling the new highway surface for the Flatbush Avenue Extension, 1924

source: Brooklyn Public Library--Brooklyn Collection. Photo by E. E. Rutter

Barren Island Factories, c. 1916

source: Brooklyn Public Library--Brooklyn Collection

FLATBUSH AVE, EXTENSION
LOOKING SOUTH TOWARD TOWARD BARREN ISLAND ON LINE OF EXT, 11/20/24 5732

Looking south toward the ferry at Barren Island along the Flatbush Avenue Extension, 1924

source: Brooklyn Public Library--Brooklyn Collection. Photo by E. E. Rutter

Aerial view of constructed jetty at Rockaway Point, 1932

source: United States Army Corps of Engineers

Aerial view of Rockaway Point, 1938

Aerial view of the future sites of the Pennsylvania Avenue and Fountain Avenue landfills, with Old Howard Beach beyond, 1938

source: New York City Parks Photo Archive

Illegal dumping in the marshes near Old Howard Beach, 1938

Aerial view of Canarsie Park, including the Coliseum roller coaster at Golden City Amusement Park, 1937

source: New York City Parks Photo Archive

View of the Albertina and Sea Bird ferries, providing service between Canarsie and Rockaway, c. 1930

source: Brooklyn Public Library--Brooklyn Collection

Aerial view looking north of Cross Bay Boulevard, connecting Broad Channel and the Raunt to Old Howard Beach, 1938

source: New York City Parks Photo Archive

Fishing at Broad Channel, c. 1915

source: Library of Congress Prints and Photographs Division

Aerial view of the Cross Bay Boulevard Bridge, looking north toward Broad Channel and the marsh islands of Jamaica Bay, 1938

source: New York City Parks Photo Archive

Cross Bay Boulevard Bridge, connecting Broad Channel with the Rockaway Peninsula, c.1938

source: Brooklyn Public Library--Brooklyn Collection

Aerial view looking east toward the Head of Bay and the future site of John F. Kennedy International Airport, 1938

source: New York City Parks Photo Archive

View of a B-36 at the International Air Exposition, New York International Airport (commonly known as Idlewild Airport), 1948

source: Port Authority of New York and New Jersey

www.ingramcontent.com/pod-product-compliance
Lightning Source LLC
Chambersburg PA
CBHW060826270326
41931CB00002B/80